Bathrooms

Bathrooms

GLOUCESTER MASSACHUSETTS

ROCKPORT

PUBLISHERS

Text: Montse Zapata
Graphic Design & Layout: Emma Termes Parera

Copyright for the international edition:
© H Kliczkowski-Onlybook, S.L.
La Fundición, 15. Polígono Industrial Santa Ana
28529 Rivas-Vaciamadrid, Madrid, Spain
Ph.: +34 91 666 50 01
Fax: +34 91 301 26 83
onlybook@onlybook.com
www.onlybook.com

Copyright for the English language edition:
© 2005 by Rockport Publishers, Inc.

Published in the United States of America by
Rockport Publishers, a member of
Quayside Publishing Group
33 Commercial Street
Gloucester, Massachusetts 01930-5089
Tel.: (978) 282-9590
Fax: (978) 283-2742
www.rockpub.com

Library of Congress Cataloging-in-Publication Data available
ISBN: 1-59253-178-4
10 9 8 7 6 5 4 3 2 1

MODERN

BATHROOMS

A modern bathroom is, perhaps, the most complicated type of bathroom to decorate. An avant-garde bathroom not only strives for beauty and visual flair, it also seeks to combine these two concepts with functional considerations. Some good opportunities can be found in a modern bathroom: experiments with new materials, mixtures of very different materials, and a practical approach to spatial arrangements. We could say that functionality and the exploitation of space and natural light are, along with innovative design, the essential characteristics of a modern bathroom. Materials such as glass and wood are fundamental: the former provides airy, luminous settings, while the latter offers warmth, comfort, and functionality. Another consideration in an avant-garde bathroom is the layout: each function has a specific area and, where there is enough space, these areas are marked off by partitions (almost always made of glass) or other elements that visually separate the different functions.

© Duccio Malagamba

© Markus Tomaselli Rataplan

© Stephen Varady and Rusell Pell

© Markus Tomaselli Rataplan

© Matteo Piazza

© Matteo Piazza

© Ross Honeysett

The exploitation of natural light is one of the main aims of modern architecture. This bathroom provides a good example with compartments made of transparent glass that allow the sunlight to penetrate the entire space.

MINIMALIST

BATHROOMS

The minimalist style can be cold and austere in a bathroom, due to the absence of any striking colors or sensuous shapes. The basis of a minimalist bathroom is the use of one or, at most, two materials, along with neutral colors, such as white and gray, and various textures of stone. This restraint is the only way to maintain the simplicity of form that is so essential to this style. Even the faucets are usually set into the wall and their design is as simple as possible.

One of the advantages of minimalism is that it conveys a great sense of order. It is, therefore, a good idea to exploit the characteristics of this style in bathrooms where space or natural light are restricted. It is also a perfect way to stress the architectural features of a space, as in the bathroom shown on this page. The absence of any bright colors or decorative details throws the spotlight onto the structure of the room, the thickness of the walls and the shape of the elements.

© Jordi Miralles

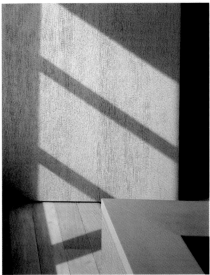

© Valerie Bennett

© Valerie Bennett

The sink and stone top comprise a single unit. A slight slope in the faucet area prevents water from spilling.

In this case, the sink is a marble tub with the faucet handle set in one side.

The bathtub has been built with the same material as the sink to emphasize the bathroom's geometric lines.

© Montse Garriga

16

© Margheritta Spiluttini

© Hélène Binet

© Jordi Miralles

Above top: In order to take full advantage of the space, the bidet and toilet have been fitted into a wall clad with wood.

Above bottom: A large rectangular mirror runs along the entire length of the wall, reflecting light on a bathroom that revolves around the contrast between black and white. The design of both the bathtub and the washbasins is extremely stark.

© Reiner Lautwein

© Reiner Lautwein

© Eugeni Pons

RUSTIC

BATHROOMS

Tiles combined with paint, or earthenware tiles matched with pebble stones are just some of the materials used to decorate rustic or Mediterranean-style bathrooms, as can be seen from the bathroom on this page. The floor is usually covered with earthenware tiles—sometimes placed loosely, unconnected by cement, or embellished with wooden inlays and decorative friezes—although we can also find wood (especially in urban settings) and concrete, either painted or in its natural color. The pebbled floors, like the one in this bathroom, are usually original, although these days a technique called imprinted cement is used to achieve an almost perfect imitation of this traditional design. The walls are clad to half their height (from 5' to 6' [1.5 to 1.8 m]) with handmade tiles, to protect the areas that come in contact with water. The rest of the wall is painted in a plain color, although sometimes special techniques are used to imitate the uneven surfaces found on the walls of old houses.

Rustic sinks are similar to those in rustic kitchens, with stone or concrete supports and tops made of natural materials.

© Pere Planells

© Pere Planells

© Pere Planells

The generous proportions of this bathroom have made it possible to create different areas: the sink and the big bathtub opposite it and, to the rear, the shower with its unclad walls. The platform with wooden planking provides access to the bathtub while dividing the space in half.

© Maite Gallardo

© Maite Gallardo

The concrete inside the shower has been clad with the same tiles as the bathtub. Only the upper part of the wall has been painted, again in green, setting it off against the bright blue of the ceiling. To the left of the shower, a toilet built into the wall, with its cistern fitted into the lower wall, adds a modern touch to this rustic style.

© Pere Planells

BATHROOMS

Integrating a bathroom into another space—normally the master bedroom—requires a large area with plenty of light. The possibilities are more limited in a confined space, and in these cases it may be better to integrate only the washbasin or bathtub and put the other elements in a separate room. An old bathtub (or a new design, in an avant garde setting) placed in the bedroom area, without any separation, works well if a strong visual impact is sought. This solution gives a space great character. Integrating the washbasin, as in the bathroom on the opposite page, can prove very practical, as it allows several people to use the bathroom facilities at the same time without disturbing each other.

In many homes, it is possible to knock down dividing walls to create bigger, loftlike spaces. This not only results in a few extra feet but also allows more sunlight to enter. This option must first be discussed with an architect, as only an expert can offer solutions for substituting the master walls of a house with some kind of pillars that ensure the stability of the architectural structure.

© Eduard Hueber

© Eduard Hueber

© Eugeni Pons

© Peter Aaron (Esto)

© Peter Aaron (Esto)

In this house, the washbasin has been installed halfway down the corridor leading to the sitting room to take advantage of spare space in the building's structure.

The wall of the corridor curves out slightly, providing space for the shower and toilet.

© Pere Planells

34

© Andreas Wagner

MATERIALS

Besides porcelain and ceramics, other materials have gained prominence in bathroom design—treated wood, steel, glass, synthetic moldings, and concrete structures—as the basic elements for delineating space. Just as kitchens have adapted to the decoration of sitting rooms, so too have bathrooms adapted to bedrooms by taking advantage of forms and materials that were once reserved for more exalted settings.

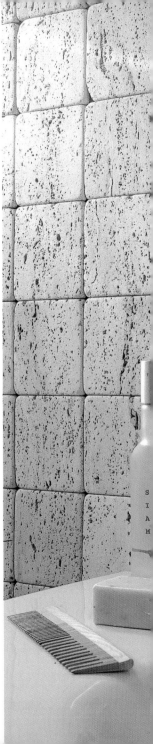

© Pablo Rojas

Mongolfiere, colorful tiles, by Bardelli

©Alvaro Gutierrez

50

COLORS

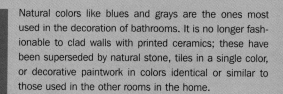

Natural colors like blues and grays are the ones most used in the decoration of bathrooms. It is no longer fashionable to clad walls with printed ceramics; these have been superseded by natural stone, tiles in a single color, or decorative paintwork in colors identical or similar to those used in the other rooms in the home.

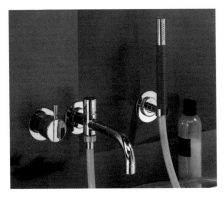

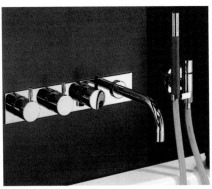

ACCESSORIES

© Happy D. by Duravit

Titanio by Flaminia

Hansgrohe by Duravit

Bol by Roca

Vero by Duravit

Serie 1930 by Duravit

Qbk by Altro

Philippe Starck Edition 1 by Duravit

Vero by Duravit

Philippe Starck Edition 1 by Duravit

Princess Yellow by Ann Sacks

Tate Deck by Ann Sacks

Reservoir by Ann Sacks

Reservoir in green by Ann Sacks

Birmingham showerhead by Ann Sacks

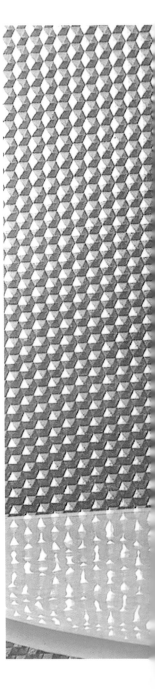

Odisea by Ramón Soler

Odisea by Ramón Soler

Benson by Ann Sacks

Tate wall mounted by Ann Sacks

One by Ann Sacks

Reservoir by Ann Sacks

Reservoir by Ann Sacks

Benson by Ann Sacks

Reservoir by Ann Sacks

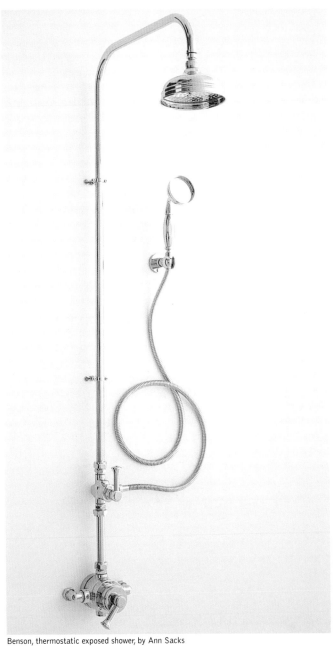

Benson, thermostatic exposed shower, by Ann Sacks

Reservoir, concealed shower, by Ann Sacks

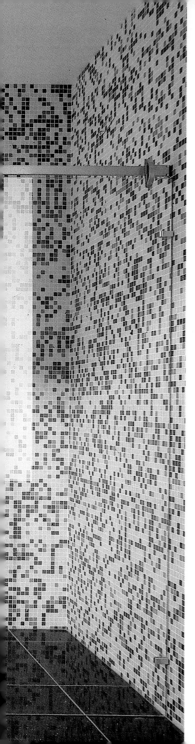

Nereus 2000, electronically controlled with 4 shower moods, by Trevi

Shower panel 5850 Classic Onyx by Formica

Shower panel 5098 Green Mistral by Formica

Chiara shower enclosure by Trevi

Talisman with Giallo by Ann Sacks

Onzen by Ann Sacks

Maillot by Ann Sacks

Princess Yellow by Ann Sacks

Lansen by Ann Sacks

85

Happy D. by Duravit

Mini Link by Flaminia

Serie 1930 by Duravit

Serie 2500 Illinois by Gedy

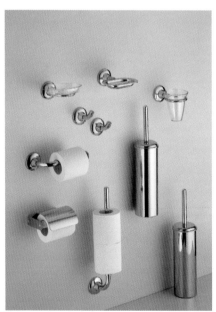

Serie 2700 Ascot by Gedy

Merdolino by Alessi

Toiletbrush Help by Gedy

Flower and Mexico by Gedy

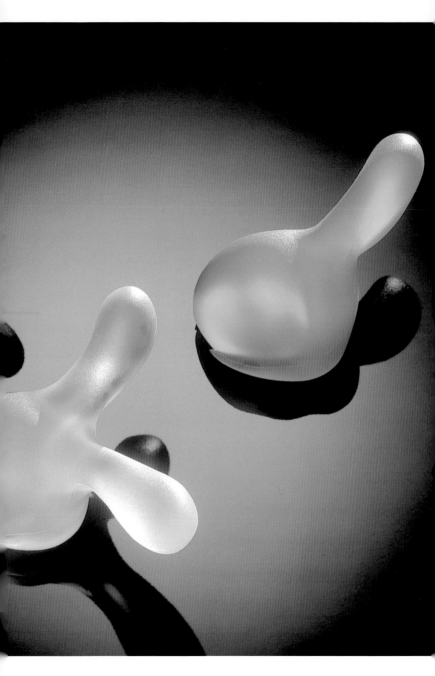

© Hinoki Soken

© Hinoki Soken

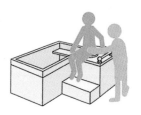

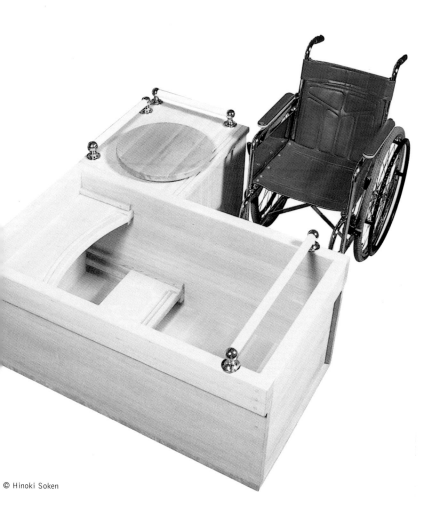

© Hinoki Soken